MAINTAIN YOUR MOMENTUM

Do Not Abandon Your God-given Purpose

Robert L. Smith

insight
PUBLISHING GROUP
Tulsa, Oklahoma

Published by Insight Publishing Group
8801 S. Yale, Suite 410
Tulsa, OK 74137
918-493-1718

Unless otherwise noted, all scripture quotations are from the Holy Bible: King James Version. Scripture quotations marked Amplified Bible are taken from the Amplified Bible copyright 1987 by The Zondervan Corporation and the Lockman Foundation.

ISBN 978-1-932503-72-2
Library of Congress catalog card number: 2007936995

Printed in the United States of America

DEDICATION

To Linda, my wife, and our sons Cedric and Justin.

CONTENTS

FOREWORD

It is my privilege to write the foreword for Robert Smith's latest book *Maintain Your Momentum*. Everything in life succeeds or fails in part because of momentum. "Big Mo" has helped people break through personal life barriers, win athletic contests, succeed in business ventures, establish life-changing ministries, and fulfill their personal destinies. Momentum can be a little mysterious. It can be positive or negative. It can work for you or work against you. However, you know when you have it, and you know when you do not. The greatest challenge for most people is how to get momentum and maintain it.

Robert Smith provides a very helpful understanding of the sources for gaining or regaining momentum and then maintaining it after you get it. *Maintain Your Momentum* is not just another self-help, personal-development book but a very practical guide, based on biblical principles, that will make a difference in your life. I believe this book will be a great encouragement and help you to fulfill your dream and destiny!

Dr. Paul Gaehring
President
Redemption Ministerial Fellowship International

ACKNOWLEDGEMENTS

I am grateful for the contribution of those who gave their time to prepare this book for publication.

Linda Smith, Alexandria, VA
Sharelene Carter, Clarksville, TN
Judith Ward, New Albany, MS
Mary Margaret King, New Albany, MS

Introduction

In life, we experience times of high energy, enthusiasm, faith, and fresh ideas. These occasions give us freshness and new hope in life. Over time, as the initial excitement fades, we subtly begin to make optional that which was once priority. The pioneering ideas we once had take a back seat to daily survival and crisis. It may be months or a year before we experience another inspiring idea and the energy to see that idea through to completion. After the inspiration and the initial enthusiasm fades, God expects us to maintain our momentum.

Momentum is defined as strength or force gained by motion or through the development of events. (Source: http://www.m-w.com/dictionary/momentum)

The Bible commands us to "Be steadfast, unmovable, always abounding in the work of the Lord, for as much as ye know that your labor [or momentum] is not in vain in the Lord" (1 Corinthians 15:58 KJV).

When you experience a boost, maintaining it is vital because maintaining it is easier than regaining it. However, you can regain your momentum if you have lost it. Make the most of opportunities and create new opportunities by being diligent. We should endeavor to maintain our momentum in prayer, believing God, faith, church attendance, giving, and loving others. Maintaining momentum has more to do with attitude than with catching a big break. It involves how you see and respond to your undesirable circumstances and environment. You may experience tough times, but you also experience opportunities to improve your situation.

Your mind is the pendulum for maintaining momentum in your life. If you maintain your mind (keep it renewed with the word of God), it will be easier to maintain your momentum. This book will help you maintain or regain your momentum. It guides you through maintaining the momentum of knowing who you are, the momentum of prayer, the momentum of gratitude, the momentum of perseverance, the momentum of being practical, and the momentum of being destiny-minded. You will receive encouragement and strength from God as you read and reread paragraphs and chapters. Some will be a home run for you while others may get you on base towards maintaining your momentum.

CHAPTER 1

THE MOMENTUM OF KNOWING WHO YOU ARE

Knowing who you are goes beyond knowing your name, culture, or occupation. It involves knowing your passions, what motivates you, and whom or what you admire. It is important to know who you are. You may have been successful in pretending to be someone you are not; but you cannot fool God, and you cannot fool yourself. Around others, you may pretend to love the things they enjoy; but both you and God know the truth about it.

Both you and God know what you sincerely enjoy and what you are really like. Once you accept who you are in Christ, you can enjoy being you. You do not have anything to prove about who you are. Others will know you by your fruit. Fruit is what you will produce season after season. There will be a pattern of consistency. Once you value who God made you to be and His purpose for your life, you can gain and maintain momentum from what He has placed in you and the direction He is guiding you.

You are who you are

By the grace of God I am what I am. (1 Corinthians 15:10 KJV)

You are who you are by the grace of God. People may not think much of you, because they may not be aware of who you are and how far you have progressed with God's help. You may not measure up to who others want you to be. Be comfortable in measuring up to being who God wants you to be. You are more than a conqueror and an overcomer by the grace of God.

You are who you are. Accept who you are. Stop trying to be someone other than who God created you to be. God's grace is designed for your weaknesses. Enough copycats exist in the world. We need more displays of originality. You are an original. Live like it.

Jesus said this about Himself, "I am."[1] He is who He is. God told Moses to tell the people that "I am has sent you."[2] Our father God is who He is. Since we are created in His image after His likeness,[3] we should be who we are (as He has created and destined us).

His Grace is sufficient for you.[4] In life you may see people who appear to be ahead of you, and you may try to be like them. If you are going to be like them, who is going to be you? God has grace for your shortcomings; His strength in you more than compensates for your inability.[5] We are not complete alone; we need God, and we need one another. I believe God

> If you insist on being someone else, who is going to be you?

will provide what you need.[6] He may not provide it to you personally; He may use someone else to help you.

Do not be too quick to dismiss people who are not like you.

You are who you are, and you should not be ashamed of it. People all over the world are desperately trying to be someone they are not. Perhaps they are impressed with someone's status or possessions. Therefore, they pursue what they see rather than pursuing who they are.

Worldly pursuits will only cause stress because they are not in accordance with God's word or grace. Only God's grace brings peace to your life. It takes significant effort to be someone else. It is enough of a challenge to be you.

The Bible teaches us in Ephesians 4:16 that the body is joined together by God. Why are so many people trying to be someone they are not? I believe it may be that they do not see their role in life as being significant or important. Perhaps they may feel as if they are a failure or their life is uninteresting. They fail to realize that they may be a vital, missing function in someone else's life. Be who God created you to be and realize that you are included in His plan.

GOD IS AN INCLUSIVE GOD

Whosoever believes in Him should not perish[7]
Whosoever calls on the name of the Lord should be saved[8]
His desire is that *all* come to repentance[9]

God goes beyond race, color, gender, or clique. He includes beyond social status or community. Sometimes God chooses someone whom people least expect. Remember what was said about Jesus' hometown:

"Can anything good come out of Nazareth?"[10] People were not accustomed to anything good coming from that location. God, who is very familiar with people and places, produces good using unlikely places and people. Some people may discriminately exclude others because of ethnicity, while God purposefully includes them regardless of ethnicity.

The root of the issue is that many people want to have economic and social status above others. Also, people want to rule over others. Unfortunately, people take advantage of and abuse others. I believe that people are the number one mentally- and physically-abused beings on earth. People are abused more than animals or the environment. Life is challenging enough as it is without having someone misuse or take advantage of you.

God wants to include everyone in His redemption plan, which is based upon His way of redemption. He does not exclude you based on what you have done or what you do not have. You can receive Jesus because He is the one who has purchased your redemption. It is His desire that none be lost, but that all come to repentance.[11] Health, wealth, peace, joy, and love accompany repentance. An invitation to receive Jesus, whom God offered up for you, demonstrates that God wants to include you. Respond to the invitation by receiving whom he offered. You are included, not excluded.

YOU ARE DISTINCT

You have received a distinct and specific assignment in life from the Lord. Do not be troubled if you are not doing what the crowd may be doing. Observe the specific assignment you have received from the Lord.[12]

He will comfort your heart in doing it as He did with Moses when he did not think he was capable of doing what God told him to do.[13]

Trust what He has placed on your heart to do. Do it with joy, enthusiasm, and love. Be proud of your purpose and calling. Do not be ashamed of it. Allow God to comfort your heart. He will give you peace in doing it.

> You are distinct, not extinct.

You need to embrace His will for your life. Seek Him to gain understanding of your purpose and destiny.

Do not allow others to make light of your purpose. It is God to whom you must give an account for the gift and calling that He has given you. God wants you to know what He created you to do and that He will help you do it.

YOU ARE HELPED BY GOD

One of your greatest attributes is to be a person whom God helps. It is your greatest virtue. God loves to help. He is in the helping business. He restores. He heals. He preserves. He saves.

Regardless of the situation or predicament you may be in, you can be helped by God. You may not know of anyone who can help you. You may think you have exhausted all of your means. You may not have anyone to whom you can turn. Turn to God.

He will help you. He loves to help you. He loves to guide you. You need help, and God is the help you need. Allow Him to fill the void you are experiencing and feeling. Allow Him to satisfy the desires which are unsatisfied.

God can and will help you. Your problem is not too big, and it is not too late. God knows what is required for your case. He knows the areas in which you need help and how to get help to you. He knows the depth of your need better than you. God loves to help you. Allow Him to help. He will help you with what plagues your mind. He will help you with your daily tasks. He will help you with receiving and giving love. He will help you with what you should say. Helping you is precious to Him. It is at the top of His agenda. He has angels who respond upon your declaration of the word of God. If you do not have a clue where your help will come from, begin saying this: "My help comes from the Lord."[14] You are not the only one who needs help, and you are not the only one He helps.

IT IS NOT ABOUT YOU

What you are going through may not be about you. The calamity in your life may not be about you. It may be necessary in order to prepare you for the people God will bless, heal, restore, and save through you.

Your focus may be on what you are going through. God's focus is on where you are going. Your focus may be on an event or something happening around you, but God's focus is on where you are going. You may be focused on your distractions, but God is focused on your destiny. Please understand that everything you go through and experience in life is not about you. The travail, beating, piercing, and death Jesus went through was not about Him; it was about us. Since He endured it for us, now it is all about Him.[15] Jesus' pain and suffering were necessary to redeem us. Since we are to fellowship with His sufferings, we will experience difficulties in life that are not about us.[16]

The devil may not be as interested in you as you may give him credit for being. His strategy is to get you focused on yourself and your personal despairs to the point that you are unable to recognize the needs of others and what you can do to help them. You are one, but you affect many. God's heart is for you to help many. Therefore, your life is about helping many. Your opinion of yourself may need to change.

> You are not a mess even though you may be experiencing one.

Your renown is not in how few troubles or problems you experience; it is in your determination and resolve to go through them and come out victoriously. You may think, "It is always something." If so, God may be allowing your experiences to develop, perfect, and polish you for future assignments. If you will be honest, you will acknowledge that the troubles you face today probably would have destroyed you a few years ago. It means that God prepared you for now. He is preparing you now for the future. Become more focused on helping others than looking for others to rescue you. You will be delivered from your own despair and realize that it is not always about you, as you participate in helping others.

The whispering and laughter of others may not be about you. Just because they are pointing in your direction, it does not mean that they are pointing at you. The meeting, which did not include you, may not have been about you. Why not believe that you were innocently overlooked? Why not believe that you were excluded because of your Godly character and integrity? You must have dynamic influence or be an awesome threat, if others go to great extent to exclude you. Perhaps you are unapproachable, or perhaps they feel that you will reject them. Perhaps you were excluded because you are the only one doing the job right. Even if witnesses say it is about you, do not always believe what they say. Be wary of anyone who is overly anxious to tell you negative things about yourself. They (the talebearers) may be the real problem.[17] Nevertheless, you have too much to accomplish to be sidetracked by anyone. Your work is meant to influence and flow into the lives of others.

YOUR HAVE AN OVERFLOW

"My cup runneth over."[18]

There is an area in your life God has anointed to be overflowing. It may be in something you do with your hands, something you do with your voice, something you do with your feet, or some kind of knowledge you possess. Nevertheless, God has destined an area of your life to be overflowing. God loves to pour—not drizzle—His blessings and favor on you. Let us review examples in scripture.

My cup runneth *over.* (Psalm 23:5 KJV)

I will *pour* you out a blessing that there will not be room enough to receive. (Malachi 3:10 KJV)

Pour out into all these vessels. (2 Kings 4:4 KJV)

Running *over* shall men give into your bosom. (Luke 6:38 KJV)

The Amplified Bible amplifies Zechariah 4: 6 this way: "causing it to yield a *ceaseless* supply of oil from the olive trees."

In light of these scriptures, there maybe an area or areas of your life where you should be expecting, saying, and experiencing overflow. There are reservoirs in your life that are meant to be an endless supply for others. Discover where they are and enjoy the overflow. Expect an overflow. You have His word on it.

YOU HAVE HIS WORD

He sent His word and healed them, and delivered them from their destruction. (Psalm 107:20 KJV)

So shall my word be that goes forth out of my mouth: it shall not return unto me void, but it shall accomplish that which I please, and it shall prosper in the thing whereto I sent it. (Isaiah 55:11 KJV)

The most effective, productive, and fruitful thing that can happen to you is for God to send His word. His word is how He operates. When He decided to save you, deliver you, prosper you, and heal you, He sent His word.[19] When His word comes into your life, it is as if He is coming Himself because He is His word.[20] Throughout scripture, God told (sent His word) someone to do something great (for example, Moses and Gideon) and said, "I will be with you."[21]

The word carries with it the presence of God. His might and protection accompany His word. When God sends you His word, it is a tremendous turning point in your life. Seize it! He is setting the course and pattern for your life through His word. His word is His guidance and counsel to you. His word is powerful enough to enable you to accomplish what it says. The resources needed to accomplish every task are within His word. Hold fast to the word and act on it (believe it) and the resources will come. As you take action in faith, you are moving in the authority of the sender of the word.

God's words are spirit and life.[22] That means that His word is more than idle or dormant rhetoric. There is life in God's word.[23] There is life within His word to produce what it says. Words have a profound effect upon our lives. We have progressed or failed to progress because of words we or someone else said about us. Wake up when God's word comes to you! I say again, it is a profound moment and turning point in your life. Do not daydream or take lightly the word of God coming from your pastor and others God has sent to speak into your life.

God's word sent to you will be timely and inspire you. It will be what you need at that moment in your life. All conditions will be right for the word to enter your life. Your heart will be prepared to receive it. God sends His word to you at the right time. Everyone around you may appear to be standing still when God sends His word to you to move forward. It may come when least expected.

Without a doubt, God's word will definitely inspire you. It will bring hope and vision. You may have been living day to day, passing the time, but the entrance of God's word brings light to dark situations.[24] It inspires you to make changes within your routine, habits, or lifestyle. It may inspire you to separate from the pack. Be excited about the word sent to you and the possibilities it brings.

You must constantly meditate upon the word and begin doing the word given to you in order to receive its benefits.[25] You need to get busy so it does not become stale or stagnant to you.[26] Do not neglect the word given to you.

Another reason He sends His word is that He desires a closer, lifelong relationship with you. God sent His word because He wants you to get to know Him better. He knows you well and wants you to know Him well. The word of God will draw you closer to Him. You must remain in communication with the sender of the word. Frequent contact with Him, through prayer, gives you the guidance you need to carry out the word given to you.

THE MOMENTUM OF PRAYER

Prayer is a catalyst when it is performed on a regular basis, with sincerity and according to God's will, which is His word. Prayer can get you started, and it is what keeps you going. For example, if prayer were an ingredient in making a cake, without it the cake would not taste right or have the proper texture. Another example would be to consider prayer in comparison to one of the body's essential vitamins. Without it, you may feel fine temporarily and no one may notice; however, over prolonged or sporadic periods you will begin to feel the effects, and it will become noticeable to others. Prayer is just that important. You need to pray every day. There are things God has lined up for you to do tomorrow, next week, next month, and next year. If you neglect prayer, you may not reach those assignments or be able to recognize key opportunities. Prayer does much more for you than you will ever recognize. There is a certain frame of mind or level of faith you need to be in next month and next year, and prayer is how you prepare for it.

Prayer is more about preparation than repair. Unfortunately, most people see prayer as a means of repairing what has gone wrong rather than preparation for things to go right. I believe the more consistent you are in prayer, the fewer repairs you will need. Not every prayer you pray needs to feel power-packed and spiritually moving. The important thing is for you to pray, both when you feel like it and when you do not. Never think or say you did not get anything out of a prayer. I believe you get something out of every prayer, whether you recognize it or not. Discipline yourself to maintain your momentum of prayer.

GIVE GOD YOUR ATTENTION

Some circumstances in your life may be God trying to get your attention. God knows you, and He knows what it takes to get your attention. What works for others may not work for you. Wake up! God may be knocking at the door of your heart.[27] He may be knocking through the circumstances you are experiencing. He may be knocking through your family, employment, or church. He used a burning bush to get Moses' attention.[28] He used a whale to get Jonah's attention.[29] He used a light from heaven to get Paul's (Saul) attention.[30] God knows you, and He knows how to get your attention. He knows how to get you in line and keep you in line. Pay attention to the still small voices in your life.[31]

> Take God off Call Waiting.

He may be trying to get you alone, get you to sit still, or get you to come aside to listen to Him. Perhaps He is using this book to get your attention. God may be getting your attention to say you are going the wrong way, there is danger ahead, you need to slow down, you are moving too fast, or to say stay firmly on course.

I do not know what God wants to tell you. It is well worth your while to give your attention to Him. You may already know what He is trying to tell you. Whatever God tells you will be consistent with scripture.

If He has your attention, let Him keep it. There may be things approaching you with the intent to draw your attention away from God. Make sure your attention is not drawn away from Him. He loves to hear from you.

SPEAK TO GOD

How many people do you speak with on a daily basis? It is an honor to have an opportunity to speak to someone in high authority. You will never be honored to speak to anyone in a higher position of authority than God. You speak to others. How about speaking to God?

A prerequisite to speaking to someone is communication (speak their language). God has identified a language for believers to communicate with Him. We communicate with Him using His word. The Bible tells us that when we petition Him according to His will (word), He hears us.[32] Moreover, since we know that He hears us, we know that we have the petition. We have a right to ask and expect what is written in His word (1 John 5:14-15 KJV).

The word also tells us that we can speak to Him in a way that no man understands but Him. What an awesome privilege! The Bible tells us in 1 Corinthians 14:2 that when we pray in an unknown tongue, we speak to God and not to men. Praying in tongues is God's frequency for the believer. It is a communications frequency, established by God, inaugurated on the day of Pentecost (Acts 2:1-4). If you want to pray to God on a level beyond your intellect, pray in tongues. Sometimes we do not know what we need to pray for or how we should pray. We may not know what God wants us to say at that time; if we pray in tongues, we are on safer ground. Praying in tongues prevents us from praying personal preferences or motives. Praying in tongues enables us to filter out what we're experiencing, which may be of secondary importance to God's plan at that moment. Praying in tongues is an act of humility towards God. It indicates that we are more interested in speaking to Him rather than getting Him to do something for us. Does it irritate you when people do not speak to you until they want something? When we pray in tongues, it decreases selfish agendas. What God desires is more important.

You always want to hear from God. God wants to hear from you also, other than when you want something. God wants to hear from you, especially when you pray in tongues. I can imagine God and Jesus having a conversation. God says to Jesus, "I have not heard from my children. Have you heard from them?" Jesus responds, "No, Father, I have not heard from them since they received money, clothes, and peace."

Speak up! God is listening.

Build yourself up![33] God knew that you would not always have people around you to build you up. He knew that there would be times when others could not build you up. He knew that there would be times when only you knew what was going on inside of you.[34] For such occasions, you may need to build yourself up. You can always build yourself up, regardless of how frequently you are downtrodden. There is a level of faith in God you need to obtain. Pray in tongues and build towards that level. As you are praying in the spirit (tongues), you are pressing your way through. Use what God has made available and given to you. Pray! Pray! Pray!

BATHE IT IN PRAYER

There are things in our lives that we need to "bathe in prayer." By bathing something in prayer, you commit to consistent and persistent prayer. There are people and circumstances over which we need to consistently pray the word of God. After the initial prayer, we need to be persistent in thanking God for having answered it.[35] Our desire for answers to prayers should be matched by our corresponding persistence in praying.

There are some things we need to allow to soak in prayer. We have soaked much in our tears. Now we need to ensure those same concerns become soaked with our prayers. To soak something is to allow it to sit in a solution for a period of time. The more we pray, the less likely we are to quit.[36]

Do not assume that it is someone else's responsibility to pray for your situation. It is your personal responsibility. It is a good thing to have others praying with you and for you. However, you need to have the attitude that you are going to pray it through if no one else ever prays about it. If you ask someone else to pray for you, be specific in your request. Tell them your desired outcome based on the word of God. Do not assume they know. They may pray for an answer while you are asking God for a different outcome.

Do not wait until you get to church to pray about it. Pray about it now and consistently. You are the one most intimately involved in your circumstance. Therefore, no one else can pray as passionately about it as you. Prayer is a responsibility as much as it is a duty. You should have confidence in your prayers.

> This is the confidence that we have in Him, that, if we ask anything according to His will, He hears us: whatever we ask, we know that we have the petitions that we asked of Him (1 John 5:14-15 KJV).

Bathing in prayer is a purposeful and conscious effort. It focuses God's attention on what has gotten our attention. Here is the process: things distract our attention. We give our attention to God. God gives us His attention. God attends to the things that distract our attention.

Your breakthrough may be as near as getting on your knees about your circumstances in prayer. Prayer can break things loose for you. Praying God's word produces results. It is one of the most powerful things you can do. God has given you the authority to break things through for yourself.

When you think about it, pray about it.

Whatever you are praying about, ensure every aspect of it is bathed in prayer. Be determined to pray about it without ceasing.[371] See it through by praying it through. Keep it in God's hands and allow Him an opportunity to fix it.

LET GOD FIX IT

Maintenance means to maintain, which is to keep up or preserve in good condition. Automobiles require regular maintenance. They require periodic oil and filter changes and tune-ups. Brake shoes, tires, wiper blades, and batteries require replacing when their effectiveness diminishes. If we fail to do the proper maintenance, we can jeopardize the longevity of the vehicle and the safety of the occupants. Maintenance on vehicles is projected and scheduled by time or mileage. We pay a significant amount of money for our cars. Therefore, it is wise for us to preserve our investment.

Some abuse their automobiles, and when they experience a problem, they take them to the repair facility and say, "Do what you can to get me back on the road—because I need my wheels." People do likewise with their lives. They abuse themselves to the point of breakdown and go to God for Him to get them back on their feet. When we do this with our cars, the repairs are more costly to us. When we do this with our lives, the repairs are more costly to us. When we do this with our cars, the garage has to keep it longer because the repair time is longer. When we do this with our lives, God has to deal with us longer to get us to the condition He desires. At the garage, we get upset when it is not an inexpensive quick fix, and we take our vehicle elsewhere. Likewise, with our lives, we get upset with God, and we look for a god of convenience.

Our lives require regular, scheduled spiritual maintenance in order to preserve us in good condition. You may assume your life is good to go, even though sometimes, like an automobile, you are hard to start and run rough. You coast into the service station (church) for a quick fix, and you are back on the road again. You know you need a tune-up, but you blame it on bad fuel (someone else). One day God may require you to make a long journey at a moment's notice. There may not be time for a tune-up. The maintenance will need to have been done. Perhaps He is ready to equip you for the trip.

We require the word of God and prayer frequently (daily). We require giving praise and worship to God. Our soul thirsts for God.[38] The center of our being hungers and thirsts after God.

At regular intervals, to avoid major breakdowns, we should repent of sin and forgive others because God has forgiven us, and we should love our enemies.[39] God is love, and He wants us to love others and develop our intimacy with Him.

INTIMACY WITH GOD

God is a God of intimacy. He longs for moments of intimacy with you. He cherishes and protects it; so must you. Intimacy means to share conversation and activities which are exclusively between you and God. Do not disclose your intimacy with God to the public. There are moments you experience with God that only you and He can appreciate. Others cannot grasp your intimacy with God. They must grasp their own.

There are secret songs sung to God and secret things whispered which are only for Him to hear. When you are in the middle of an intimate moment with God, do not spoil it by thinking and saying to yourself, "I can't wait to tell someone about this." There are songs you sing to God which are soothing to His ear, but others would laugh and mock you if you told them.

There are moments with God that the only thing you can do is cry. Others may not have an appreciation for it, but God values it. Keep and preserve your intimacy with God. Your fellowship with Him is personal. There are times during your intimacy that He tells you things to share with others. Do so without disclosing your personal level of intimacy.

God wants you to love Him with all your heart, soul, mind, and strength.[40] If you love Him to this degree, there will be much intimacy and prayer for others. Keep it intimate!

PRAY FOR PEOPLE

We should pray for people more than we pray for things. Pray for people you know. Pray for the individual. Ask God to guide them, preserve them, restore them, or save them. If a crime has been committed in your area, ask God to save the criminal(s). If there is poverty in your area, ask God to prosper the poor.[41] If there is violence in your area, ask God to give peace to the violent. If there is corruption in your environment, ask God to correct the corrupt. Whatever you do, pray for people!

Do you pray for things you desire or possess more than you pray for yourself? Ask God to help you, regardless of how helpless or strong you feel. Ask God to give you new ideas and concepts which will be of great benefit for you and others. Thank Him for giving you your individual uniqueness. Thank God for what you have and what you have achieved. Thank God for your life.

You add value to the earth (the place). Your existence adds value to the lives of others. How would you feel if someone told you that you are replaceable? When people say this, they are referring to what you do (things) instead of who you are (the person). You are not replaceable. You bring more to your family, community, job, and society than the activities you do for them. You mean more to God than you know. God so loved the world (the people).[42] Unfortunately, some people so love the world (the places and things) until they are giving their lives for it. You have a friend (Jesus) who laid down His life for you (the person).[43] Pray for people more than you pray for things; in doing so, you show respect and gratitude towards God.

CHAPTER 3

THE MOMENTUM OF GRATITUDE

I believe that grateful people experience a greater number of God's peace and blessing than ungrateful people. People who are grateful attract the favor of God and the favor of others. They are as grateful for you passing them the saltshaker as they are for you surprising them with their heart's desire on their birthday.

We are all grateful about something in some way. We may not express it or say it. Yet, there is something in life for which you should be grateful to God. The important thing is to express your gratitude to God about that one thing and build upon it by adding others as you think of them. I encourage you to stop what you are doing and call someone to thank them for something they said or did for you. Also, take the time to thank God for what He does for you every day.

Gratitude should be a part of your prayer to God. Gratitude should be a part of your daily conversation towards and to your spouse and children. Make it a point to call, write, email, or text people who have done things for you and have helped you. Chances are God put it on their hearts to do so. Thank them and God. This is not a once-in-a-lifetime event. Make gratitude a way of life.

The Eyes of Gratitude

I believe that it is spiritually healthy for us to see people through eyes of gratitude. Unfortunately, some people see things and others through eyes of malice or disdain. The way in which we see things and people with gratitude can do wonders for our outlook and progress in life.

God uses people who seem to possess little to do great things for others. He uses parents, relatives, neighbors, and friends to do what seems impossible. There are many people unnoticed in the public eye, who work miracles day after day, raising children and working laborious jobs, and they never complain. These people are seasoned in durability and persistence. Quitting and giving up is not in their vocabulary. They do not need anyone to encourage them, nor do they seek anyone to give them accolades. We thank God for these people and the positive impact they have on others. These people may be parents, grandparents, uncles, aunts, or friends. Appreciate neighbors or strangers who have helped you and have been concerned about your well-being.

Thank God for caring people who genuinely care for your life and will not put you down so they can get ahead — people who are willing to stick with you. Thank God for them.

Be grateful for people who are key in your life but who may not be in the news or "in the know." Someone may not be well-known or known at all. I believe that as we are grateful for those who help us, we express gratitude towards God. There are people in your life who will benefit from you seeing them through eyes of gratitude. Acknowledge God's grace on their lives.

Value God's Grace

There are several things in life we value. We may value our loved ones, homes, jobs, and possessions. These are things we see and others see. God wants us to also value something He has given to us, which is not always visible. He wants us to value His grace.

God's grace is manifested in different ways. The ability or talent we see in people may be the grace of God. In some, His grace may be knowledge and wisdom. In others, it may be their ability with children. In some, it is their ability to solve complex problems. In others, it is His wise counsel in them. In some, it is His grace to sing, teach, or preach. In others, it is His athletic ability. In some, it is His ability to build and construct. In others, it is His artistic and creative ability. In some, it is His ability to govern or lead. I may or may not have mentioned your area, but God has given grace to you.

We should value the grace God has given us. This becomes a challenge because the inclination of people is to take individual credit for their accomplishments. Others idolize and worship them because of their accomplishments without realizing that they were done by the grace of God. God is a jealous God and wants us to acknowledge Him.[44]

You are who you are by the grace of God.[45] Since God has given you His grace, it means that there is something He wants you to do that you cannot accomplish on your own. When you see others doing magnificent things in God, know that they are who they are by the grace of God. Knowing this will help you realize that you can do great things too, by the grace of God.

God's grace is sufficient.[46] Some things you cannot do on your own without God. His grace supplies the sufficient knowledge, education, strength, patience, endurance, and peace to do it.

His strength is made perfect in weakness.[47] There are areas in your life where you feel as though you are weak. You may think this weakness is limiting you from doing what you need to do. God's grace is made for your weakness. The weakness may still be there, but His grace is also still there. There is grace custom-made for your weakness.

His grace given to me was not in vain.[48] Responsibility accompanies grace. To whom much is given, much is required.[49] There is work involved. Do not allow the grace of God on your life to become dormant. Work it! Use what He's given you.

Do not frustrate the grace of God.[50] Do not ignore the grace of God in your life. Apprehend it! Use it! Appreciate it! Flow with it! Flow in it! I believe the number one thing that frustrates the grace of God is when you try to be someone other than or do something other than what God purposes you to be or do.

God gives more grace to the humble.[51] It takes humility to obey the word of God (be a doer of the word). Allow me to say it another way. I believe that humility is you realizing that it is God, acknowledging that it is God, and depending upon God. If you want to experience more of the grace of God in your life, be humble. Regardless of how much grace you have, you need more in order to persevere.

CHAPTER 4

THE MOMENTUM OF PERSEVERANCE

You are not going to experience immediate success in every endeavor in life. There will be days, weeks, and months in which you may ask yourself, "What is the use?" There will be times when it may appear that you are accomplishing nothing, even though you are diligent. This is why there is a word called "perseverance." Perseverance is not for when things are smooth and easy and when everything you touch immediately turns to gold. It is for when it seems like there is only you and God, and you wonder where He is.

Keep up the pace even though you do not see the finish line. Keep your form even though you are tired. Tell yourself you can do it when no one else is cheering you on. You may have told yourself that since you are in last place and far behind the pack that if you quit, no one will notice, and no one will care. God cares. He wants you to persevere. There will be times that both your mind and your body will tell you to quit. Challenge yourself to persevere. Once you do so, you will gain momentum that spills over into several areas in your life. In the future, if you are thinking about quitting or giving up, read this book repeatedly — especially this chapter.

WHATEVER IT TAKES TO PERSEVERE

What we do and how we react (or respond) to a given situation depends upon our personal level of faith, courage, belief, or conviction. How I apply myself in a situation will be (and should be) different from how you apply yourself in a similar situation.

When Jesus told His disciples, "Let us go to the other side," and a storm arose, it caused His disciples to respond differently than He. He rebuked them for their response (lack of faith).[52] Many of us act similarly to Jesus' disciples about various situations in our lives. We are saying, "Do not you care that I am in this mess?"[53] We are saying it by our actions (or lack of actions), by our looks of self-pity, by our sarcastic statements, or by our talk of demise. We should respond in faith. However, our faith response may be different from that of others.

Allow me to explain what I mean. In a given situation, you may have enough faith to get through it without praying about it. Conversely, I may need to pray night and day to get through the same situation. In a given situation, you may be able to handle it on your own, not needing assistance. I, on the other hand, may need the assistance of two or three people to get through the same situation. An allergic reaction is another example. Some people may be able to wallow in a bed of hay without sneezing. You may start sneezing at the mention of hay. Some people can be skyscraper window washers. Others become nervous if they're on an elevator beyond the second floor.

We have internal signals, calibrated to guide us. We need to pay attention to our individual signals. Two people may be faced with the opportunity to do an illegal activity. One person may do it without thinking twice (hopefully not). The other person may become unsettled at the thought of it. A person may be willing to pay two thousand dollars for a suit, it being the dollar value they place on their attire. On the other hand, another person may not be willing to spend two thousand dollars on their entire wardrobe.

Let the peace of God guide you (your internal signal).[54] God knows you better than you know yourself. If you are willing and allow Him, He will guide you. You need to do whatever it takes for you personally to persevere and be successful, without harming others or breaking the law. You may need to work harder to get ahead as long as your compensation is proper. You may need to apologize to someone and ask for their forgiveness, even if they do not do the same. You may need to go the extra mile with someone (be more patient with them). You may need to lend a helping hand, although no one else is helping. You may need to correct someone whom everyone else is fearful of approaching, although they agree that correction is needed.

Much of whatever it takes depends upon how prepared we are. The more we believe and do what the word of God says, the more we will be able to maintain victory over life's challenges. Preparation in the word of God is an indi-

> God expects us to be diligent (persevere) based upon the ability He has given us. (Matthew 25:14-30 KJV)

vidual thing; it hinges on individual application and commitment. The significance of the word of God to us individually depends upon what we believe and how we think. Some people may become grounded in the word by spending five hours a week in the word, although others may need ten hours. The important thing is to do what it takes for you personally. Although you may think you cannot, if you persevere God will reward you.

WHEN IT SEEMS LIKE YOU CANNOT, THAT IS WHEN YOU CAN

God always causes us to triumph in Christ.
(2 Corinthians 2:14 KJV)

Many times in life, it seems as though we are incapable and unable to achieve our goals or fulfill our purpose. Sometimes, it seems as though things are getting worse, instead of better. Oftentimes it seems as if it is hopeless and useless. The strongest of believers may have such moments of doubt and despondence. During these times when we seem our weakest, I believe we may be at one of our strongest points. Too often we mistakenly compare our lives with that of someone else and our progress to that of others, forgetting that we have an individual path, season, and destiny which may appear to be similar to others' but is distinct for us. I am glad God made us. He made us with individual qualities, features, and capabilities. Therefore, it takes individual preparation to craft us into our bent or purpose in life.

Every "I can" began as "I cannot." Everything that we now can do once was a "can not do" for us. There was a time we could not walk, talk, or feed ourselves, and now we can. There was a time we could not read or communicate, but now we can. As we patiently continued on the path of personal development, the things we once could not do, we can now do. Likewise, if we persist, today's "cannot do" will become a "can do." We did not begin walking or talking at the same time or rate as other children. In the right timing for us, we began. As you were beginning to learn to ride a bike, you fell, crashed, and seemed to be out of control. Why? You were in the stage of conquering your fear or your inability to ride a bike. Usually we learn the "how to" process best when we are left alone to patiently persevere.

There may be things (goals, tasks) that it seems you cannot do. It is a matter of time and persistence before you realize that you can. There are obstacles in your path today that are telling you, "You will never get by me!" Some of you have told yourselves that this is as far as I can go. If this describes you, begin to fight back with your faith.

THE FIGHT IS NOT OVER; GET UP

Fight the good fight of faith.
(1 Timothy 6:12 KJV)

Many people have been knocked down in life; and they remain there, not trying to get up because they think the fight is over. You are only in the sixth round of a twelve-round fight. GET UP! God knows how long your battle should last. He created you with the endurance to hang in there.

You may have been punched or knocked down in life, but you must get up. The blows may have been so severe that your vision and senses are blurred. Refuse to be counted out. You may be hit again, but do not allow the fact that you have been hit to keep you down.

Yes, you may be ashamed because life has knocked you down. OK, you are down. Others see you down, but they will be impressed if you get up. In life you are going to have moments of shame, but they should be temporary and not permanent.

Some people fall down intentionally in an attempt to shorten the round. The fight is not over; keep fighting! Your getting up is not all about you. It is for the benefit of others who will witness you getting up and those whom you will be able to tell not to throw in the towel. Resume the fight!

> God is counting on you, not counting you out.

DO NOT STOP RUNNING

The race (of life) is not given to the swift or to the strong, but to him who endures to the end. You are running in life if you are alive. Stop running from life and continue to run in life. You may feel weak, incapable, ineffective, or confused, but do not stop running. Your run may be life itself or your marriage, children, health, job, ministry, finances, or relationship with God. God will strengthen you if you do not stop running.

Sure, your run has been far from perfect, and it has been laced with pain and sorrow. Nevertheless, you are still in it. Your run has enormous competition. Daily, you face numerous things competing for your time, attention, money, emotions, mind, and energy.

You are going to surpass many obstacles and overtake many people if you keep running. Your resilience to keep running must outweigh your fear of the obstacles you encounter. You will overtake many people in your path because they will slow down or stop running. Some of you may be in the fifth or last place for the moment. There will come a time when you are in the forefront if you persevere.

There is always more in you. Therefore, demand more of yourself. Expect more of yourself. Have more respect for yourself. Your age does not limit your ability to succeed. Your numerous past failures do not limit your ability to succeed. Negative comments do not limit you. Every naysayer assumes that you will not persevere. If you persevere today, tomorrow you will be glad you did. If you endure this year, next year you will be glad you did.

Keep running, although most of your run has been uphill or through storms. You need to tell yourself and continue telling yourself, "I am not going to stop, I must finish." You may not have the energy or enthusiasm you once had, but keeping running. Do you realize that many people respect you because you are still running? Run well, and do not be hindered! [55]

IN ALL THESE THINGS

In all these things we are more than conquerors through Him that loved us. (Romans 8:37 KJV)

You are more than a conqueror. Right now! While you are reading this, you are more than a conqueror. Right in the middle of your crisis, despair, need, hurt, failure, and weakness, you are more than a conqueror.

The Word says "in all these things." In all your things. Your thing may be joblessness, lack, or fear. Nevertheless, you are more than a conqueror while you are in it. Do not wait until things improve before you say you are more than a conqueror. Say it now!

In your mess, you are more than a conqueror. In your tears, you are more than a conqueror. Surrounded by enemies, you are more than a conqueror. Trouble on every side, you are more than a conqueror. You may have lost the will to fight, but you are still more than a conqueror. Everyone around you may have given up on you, and you may have given up on yourself; you are still more than a conqueror. Right now!

It is one thing to be a conqueror, but you have exceeded that. You are more than a conqueror. Perhaps you have wanted to be a conqueror, but you are more than that. A conqueror is someone who always wins, one who always triumphs. It is someone who perseveres until victory is achieved. Yet you are more than that because you are more than a conqueror. You exceed conqueror status. The unique thing about it is that you are that way now, in all things.

I believe there is still some life in you, still some hope in you. It may be only a residue of hope, but that is enough. I believe you are worth reviving because God said, "In all these things you are more than a conqueror." God saw you in it before you got in it and said you are more than a conqueror. Therefore, while you are in it, you need to say what God said. Saying what God said will get you through it. Sure, you are in a fight. Sure, it is tough. Of course, you get weary. Yes, it has been a long time. However, your life is not wasted. You may have wasted some time and effort, but God will turn what seems a waste into a profit. God works with who you are rather than who others want you to be.

You may have allowed someone or society to identify you. They may have identified you as a statistic, has been, never was, or never will be. You may identify yourself based upon others' descriptions or opinions of you. There is no one more knowledgeable or powerful than God. He identified you. His identity of you is more than a conqueror. Notice, He did not identify what you are in or going through. He called them things, because they are inconsequential to Him in comparison to you. He is more interested in you than your dilemmas. He values you more than what you are in, what you have, or what you do not have.

The things may not be what you need to conquer. I exhort you to conquer your opinion of yourself. Start seeing yourself as more than a conqueror. Begin telling yourself that you are more than a conqueror. You are who God said you are – more than a conqueror.

Things do not define you unless you allow them to. The things you are in do not define or limit your ability. You are more than a conqueror in all these things. This includes things of the past, present, or future. You may remember the things. You may see and hear the things. You may feel the things. You are greater than the things you have experienced. At times, it may appear that things are greater than you. This also applies to good things such as possessions (jewelry, house, money, etc.) Regardless of how much you possess, your value will always be greater than the value of what you possess. Realize this and begin to see yourself more valuable than the things you desire.

God does great things with people who appear to be little or insignificant. In Judges 7:2, God told Gideon that he had too many people for him (God) to defeat the enemy. Sometimes we try to defeat the enemy with an abundance of things. Families and parents may feel that they are successful because they are always on the go or "in the know." It is not about our might but God's might. As with Gideon, sometimes God may allow you to become outnumbered (overwhelmed) before He shows Himself strong.

You and God alone will always have overwhelming odds in your favor. I believe God never gives up on you. However, He may wait until you give up before He speaks or intervenes. In the eyes of God, it may be a good thing for us to be at our wits' end. God is wiser than men.[56] Therefore, no matter how formidable (wise) you think you are or your opposition is, God is much wiser.

Sometimes our vision is limited by what we experience (environment). There is always a way out and a way through, and God knows it. He sees where you are and your way through. As you believe and realize that God desires and can lead you through, you will begin to discover your way through. You are a conqueror right now where you are, in all these things in your life.

ENDURE FOR A NIGHT

Weeping may endure for a night but joy comes in the morning. (Psalm 30:5 KJV)

It is not a tragedy if you are weeping. You may not be weeping literally. However, you may be weeping (or in despair) because of failure, your children, your finances, your health, your relationships, or your employment. We all weep at some point in life about something. You may be weeping, but you need to *endure for a night.* The night is a season. It is unpleasant and undesirable. Your night may be a week, a month, or a year. God is telling you to endure for a night (season). Women who are pregnant endure for a season (nine months). Runners who are competing in a race endure for a season. Jesus endured for a season "for the joy that was set before Him, He endured the cross, despising the shame."[57] Always remember that what you are experiencing or going through is only for a night (season).

God knew beforehand that you would have some nights (dark times) in your life. He wrote instructions for the night. His instructions do not say, "Because it is night, I authorize you to quit." He does not say, "Talk about how dark and dismal your night is." In fact, He said to do the opposite. He said to endure. Since He is God and He said to endure, you should and can endure. He is expecting you to endure. Expect yourself to endure.

You may be praying for God to remove the night (adversity). Consider praying for endurance through the adversity. Some people will have a heavy object in their paths and wish they had someone to move it for them, instead of desiring the strength to move it themselves. Pray for endurance and perseverance. Become a person with great perseverance. Be determined to be determined.

Your enduring is important. It may determine the level of your future joy or if you will have similar experiences. Have an enduring attitude. Be grateful to God. Do not become weary in well doing for in due season you will reap if you do not faint.[58]

We sleep at night. Unfortunately, some people do the same thing during seasons in their lives. Do not allow this to be you. To overcome in your life, all you need to do is endure the nights.

GET BACK ON YOUR FEET

The Lord specializes in getting people back on their feet. He is an expert in helping people make a comeback. He is perfect in all His ways. Therefore, He can get you back up on your feet in life. Allow me to explain this further. Jesus said this about Himself, "I am the resurrection and the life: he that believes in me, though he were dead, yet shall he live".[59]

Jesus is the resurrection. He rose (got up) from His most adverse situation. So can you. His situation appeared to be hopeless, but He got up. So can you. In fact, He expects you to get up. He is waiting for you to get up. He is standing by to help you rise up in life. You have our example of resurrection willing to help you get up.

Some mourned while others celebrated His demise. Someone may be mourning over or laughing at you in your situation. What others said or believed did not prevent Jesus from getting up. What others are saying or have said about you should not prevent you from getting up (making a comeback).

Although He was dead, He is alive. Although your hope may seem dead, it can be revived. Believe God and allow Him to revive your life. Others who have witnessed both your despair and your revival will see what God can do. You may know someone who needs to hear that they can get up and that Jesus specialized in helping people rise up in life. Use this chapter to encourage others that they can get up (make a comeback). Help them up.

YOU ALWAYS HAVE HELP

"And I will ask the Father, and He will give you another Comforter (Counselor, Helper, Intercessor, Advocate, Strengthener, and Standby) that He may remain with you forever."
(John 14:16 AMP)

The Holy Spirit is with us and in us.[60] He also abides with us forever.[61] Therefore, He is who we have with and in us forever. We have the comforter (who is our Counselor, Comforter, Helper, Strengthener). We always have the Holy Spirit present to do these things in us and for us because we need comfort, help, strength, etc. Since He made us, He knows what He made us for in life.[62] He will guide us into the truth of what He made us to do in life and into the truth about life.[63] Therefore, He will comfort, counsel, help, and strengthen you in and towards pursuing and doing what He planned and purposed for your life. Consequently, in this area of your life you will have His extraordinary comfort, counsel, help, and strength to get you there and to keep you in the path He desires. He will lead you in this direction through His comforting, counseling, helping, and strengthening. He enables you in this area and path of your life. You have divine enablement. What is His motive for giving this to you? It is for you to help others. Likewise, this should be your motive, realizing who gave it to you and why it was given to you.

The Holy Sprit will always enable (comfort, counsel, help, and strengthen) us to help (serve) others, using the ability He has given us. What areas in your life has He comforted, counseled, helped, and strengthened? He has helped and is helping you to help others. For example, this book consists of chapters He has given me, but it is not only for me; it is to help others. He revealed it to me to help, counsel, strengthen, and comfort others.

God will work in and through us to achieve victory and success. He will strengthen us to overcome all opposition, discouragement, and setbacks. He will counsel us in how to do it. He will comfort us in times of need. That is why the Bible says, "If this counsel or work be of men it will come to naught; but if it be of God you cannot overthrow it; lest haply you be found even to fight against God" (Acts 5:38-39 KJV).

What seems to come naturally may actually be coming supernaturally from the Holy Spirit. His comfort, counsel, help, and strength will be consistent with His design and plan for your life. You will not be everything for everyone, but you will be and you are something to someone - to those who God has assigned you to help. You will not succeed at everything, but there is something at which the Holy Spirit will help you be successful and which you will enjoy.

YOU ARE STRONGER NOW THAN YOU HAVE EVER BEEN

You are stronger now than you have ever been. You are strong in the Lord and in the power of His might.[64] It may not seem like it and you may not feel like it, but you are stronger than you were last year. Outwardly, you may seem to be to perishing, but inwardly you are being renewed day by day according to God's word.[65] The adversities you faced this year might have devastated you last year. You are able to do more conquering this year because of what you overcame last year. You are able to begin new tasks this year that you did not have the heart to attempt last year. You are stronger now than you have ever been. You discern more now than you have before. You are wiser this year than you were two years ago. The battles you labored over three years ago are no longer entertained. You do not fall for the same tricks and gimmicks. You have forgotten the things that once plagued your mind. You now choose your battles instead of them choosing you. The things that formerly made you fall now only make you stumble.

The word of God has more veracity and credibility with you than ever before. You are more skillful in your prayers. Your sincerity means more to you. Friendship is more valuable and critical than three years ago. People you sought as friends five years ago no longer appeal to you. You are more determined and focused on your destiny.

Your conquest over yesterday's battles prepared you for today's obstacles, making you stronger now than you have ever been.

YOU ARE PREPARED

The Lord has prepared you for this day. When He prepared you for this day, He also prepared you for the adversities of today. It is within you. The wisdom, strength, and might you need today are in you. You were prepared yesterday for today. You were prepared for today's open doors, victories, and decisions. You were prepared in the wildernesses of yesterday. The word you received yesterday (years ago, last year, and last month) was effective yesterday and is effective today, and forever.[66] Do not despair. You are prepared. You have the armor of God at your right hand and at your left hand. You shall not be moved or shaken from your place in God. Your today may have come suddenly, but you are ready for triumph and victory. I believe that the boldness of Christ is rising up within you; take your stand as one who reigns as a king in life.[67] Despair and dismay can no longer hold you captive. The fears of yesterday no longer bind you. Your wisdom exceeds that of your foes. The precision of your pursuits renders your enemy unarmed. Rise up! Rise up! You are a conqueror today, although you may have succumbed yesterday. The least of your might can defeat your greatest obstacle. You have the will to fight for what is rightfully yours, which is an abundant life.[68] You always triumph in Jesus.[69]

God always gives you the victory.[70] The one who helps and strengthens you has never forsaken you. The enemy may have tried to catch you with your guard down, but he has failed to realize that you are on the offense (always abounding) instead of retreating.[71] You have reinforcement. Your spiritual reserves (the angels) are ready and waiting for you to call them to service. They move out upon your mention of the word of God.[72] The prayers you prayed, the word you heard, and the grace you received, will endure in your life today and tomorrow.

You are prepared to handle the circumstances of your life and to help others with their circumstances. Use what God has given you. Believe in God and believe in yourself. God is patient with you. Be patient with yourself. Your current status is PREPARED.

BELIEVE

In life, we should live like, pray like, endure like, and give like we believe. There needs to be a level of exertion and sense of urgency that is consistent with and indicative of the fact that we believe. Faith without works is dead.[73] Therefore, our faith needs to be visible in our living and giving. We need to pray like, teach like, and work like we believe. Coaches need to coach like they believe their team will win. The Bible tells us that we have won. We need to live like it. Singers need to sing as though they believe. Intercessors need to intercede as though they believe.

Believe the word of God.

Parents need to raise and train their children as though they believe in God. Husbands need to love their wives as though they believe what the Word says.[74] Husband and wife need to be one as though they believe what the Word says.[75] Children need to obey their parents in the Lord as though they believe the word of God.

We need to endure in life as though we believe that we are victorious. We need to reach out to others as though we believe God is using us to help them. We need to appreciate others as though God has put them in our lives for a purpose. We need not give up on those around us nor ourselves, believing that the present tribulation is a necessary part of our destiny.

We need to thank God as though we believe that He has heard and answered our prayers.[76] We need to praise God as though we believe that He has given us the victory. We need to forgive and be long-suffering with others as though we believe that God has done likewise towards us. We need to live as though we believe that Jesus is coming soon. We need to live as though we believe that God is holy and we should be holy.[77] Practice these things in your life (be practical).

CHAPTER 5

THE MOMENTUM OF BEING PRACTICAL

The Bible tells us that we have this treasure in earthen vessels.[78] That means that we are not exempt from the challenges, distractions, and schemes in life. While we are to be diligent in doing the spiritual activities required of us, we are also to be of a sober, balanced mind. We are to be aware that we may be considered vulnerable targets for schemers because we are believers; therefore, some people may view us as being naïve and gullible. As believers, we are to be wise and alert to guard against such, and at the same time, take full advantage of the opportunities and benefits available as citizens of our country. Likewise, we must understand that we will reap what we sow.

Our spiritually vulnerable areas may be the areas that we think are the least likely targets. It may be an area or activity which we think will not do us any harm because it is small in magnitude or unnoticeable at the current time. It may be developing an ill-advised habit or omitting a habit that is life-sustaining. These things usually begin subtly and gain momentum as we continue to maintain or neglect certain activities.

LITTLE - DO YOU REALIZE

A *little* leaven leavens the whole lump.
(1 Corinthians 5:6 KJV)

The *little* foxes that spoil the vine.
(Song of Solomon 2:15 KJV)

This chapter reveals a strategy of your adversary, the devil (1 Peter 5:8). When he embarks on destroying your marriage, finances, relationships, health, or ministry, he uses one of his covert workers, called "little." He knows that you may not commit a lot of sin, but you may indulge in a little. He knows you may not involve yourself in a lot of confusion, but you may instigate a little. He knows you may not participate in a lot of backsliding, but you may allow a little. He knows that you may not kill anyone with a gun, but you may kill a little with your words. He knows you may not agree to a divorce, but you may consent to a little break in communication with your spouse. He knows that you may not use a lot of profanity, but you may use a little. Do you get the point?

Therefore, a covert agent of the devil called "little" is seeking to get in or is already in your life. Perhaps he has befriended you by convincing you that you have a right to give a little. Little suggests, "Concerning this tithe thing, you do not need to give ten percent, just as long as you give a little." Do you realize how big a problem little is causing you? Can you afford to have an "ignore it, it is only a little" attitude? Do not ignore the little things in your life, which may lead you off track. The following is how the word of God refers to the devil.

They that see thee shall narrowly look upon thee, and consider thee, saying, Is this the man that made the earth to tremble, that did shake kingdoms. (Isaiah 14:16 KJV)

THERE IS A REASON FOR ALL OF THIS

There is a reason for all of the calamity, confusion, and constant need. What you experience from day to day may not be coincidental. There is a reason for repeated cycles, seasons, and lessons in life. God is always preparing and developing us for the future. The current season may occupy our attention, but our future and destiny is what God is focused on. He knows what we need for our destiny. Therefore, do not get overly upset about what you are going through.

You may be passing through one of life's storms. I believe that our journey in life will lead us through storms, as opposed to us being stationary in life, with the storms coming to us. Nevertheless, there is a reason for all this. Life has much to do with cause and effect. If our effects are undesirable and out of God's will, we need to consider the cause by considering our ways.[79]

It is frustrating to consistently experience the same old things. Consider what you are doing that may be allowing it or what you are not doing that could change it. It may be you, your environment, associations, or beliefs. Working on the reason (cause) requires daily diligence and discipline. You have to make it a point and priority to work on it. Focus on the dividend (results) rather than the investment (daily effort). There is a reason for this writing. I believe the reason is to strengthen you and others.

Small things become great

Small and simple routines in life produce great and significant results over time. Sometimes we put pressure on ourselves to always hit a home run. What we may need to do is to keep getting on base. If we keep hitting singles, doubles, or triples, it will add up to much at the end of the season.

Some people do not try because they do not believe they can hit a home run, so they do not consider a single. Somewhere, in some way, you are hitting a single in your life, and you have counted it as insignificant. The small good and godly things you do will make a big difference in your life. You may have struck out the last time you tried to do right. At least you tried. Try again! The seemingly little things you do for your spouse, children, friend, or neighbor make a big difference.

You have struggles and challenges that you thought you would never face in your life. Your persistence through them is making a difference for you and for those who know you. Do not try to bite off more than you can chew. Do the things you can do and be faithful in doing them. As you do this, the amount you can chew will increase. Something as simple as a phone call or visit goes a long way. Your small ideas may be worth thousands and millions of dollars. Work your seemingly small contributions with diligence. Your contributions are significant. Use the faith you have and do not try to use someone else's faith.

CAN YOU AFFORD THAT?

Live by faith and not by sight.
(2 Corinthians 5:7 KJV)

Can you afford to live by sight rather than by faith? It is too expensive and too costly to live by sight. It will consume most of your energy, time, and finances to live by sight, even though it will initially look like you are doing the right thing. Living by sight far exceeds your budget. It exceeds your spiritual, mental, and financial income. Living by sight is too expensive to maintain. Living by sight is beyond your means.

The sight (of the man, woman, house, car, and endeavor) may be far beyond your means. The interest you will pay on that relationship you are establishing by sight is astronomically high. It may take years for you to rid yourself of its debt. Are you sure you can afford to walk by sight? Is what you see (by sight) really what you are getting or what you want?

In order to live by sight, you may have to shift or divert resources (energy, time and money) from elsewhere in your life to compensate for or afford what you are attracted to by sight. Can you afford the sleep, peace, and joy it may cost you? Can you afford the confusion, discord, and despair which accompany it? Initially it may look good. Will it still look good in a year or three years? Will the sight of it disgust you in the future?

Can you afford that one-way relationship in which you are the only one giving? Can you afford to lose the good relationships, which have proved to be true? How do things look from where you are sitting, and are you looking through the eyes of faith? Take another look and ask God, "Can I afford this?" Ask God if He will provide resources for what you see.

If you obtain it by faith, you can maintain it by faith. If you begin by faith, you can complete it by faith. Faith is the one thing you can afford. The more of it you use, the more you get (we go from faith to faith). Faith does not cost; it pays. Faith pleases God, which is why He tells us to live by it and not by sight. We always have time to please God.

Do not waste time

We waste things in life from time to time. Sometimes we waste money, energy, or food. I believe, if we totaled up all the waste in our lives, our largest waste would be time. It is likely that we waste some amount of time every day. Yet, of all the things we can waste, time is the one thing we cannot restore.

I believe there are a few reasons we waste time: procrastination, lack of knowledge, or wrong associations. We waste time and waste our lives away when we continually put things off. We need to establish goals (with a plan). If we do not have a plan, which includes a schedule, we are open to procrastination. It is worth your time to write down realistic, achievable goals and apply a schedule to accomplishing your goals. Along the way, evaluate your performance and hold your own feet to the fire in ensuring that you get them done.

> For precept must be upon precept, precept upon precept: line upon line, here a little and there a little. (Isaiah 28:10 KJV)

This scripture indicates the effectiveness of persistence (staying at it). You attain progress (success) by consistent effort rather than by occasional dabs.

Better is the end of a thing than the beginning thereof. (Ecclesiastes 7:8 KJV)

Do not be discouraged by your small beginning. If you remain consistent in working at it, you will see results later. This scripture applies to the negative also. For instance, if you consistently waste time and you continue to do so, you will progressively become a better waster of time.

Lay aside the weight that so easily ensnares us. (Hebrews 12:1 KJV)

There are things (attitudes, habits, or activities) which limit your progress. They help you waste time. Do your very best, by applying the word of God, to lay aside (walk away from) whatever ensnares you.

Some people waste time because of a lack of knowledge about what they should be doing. They are unsure of what they should be doing. Therefore, they do not do anything. I believe you should do something and adjust if you have missed the mark.

Time is one thing we cannot recycle in order to conserve it. The word of God teaches us that God will redeem the time. I believe He redeems the time once we begin applying ourselves to do what we believe He desires us to do. The extra 15 minutes in the morning, during lunch, or in the evening can be dedicated to productivity. Perhaps our mistake is waiting for our entire schedule to be cleared for months on end before we decide to be more productive. Begin with the spare five minutes you have and notice the results. I challenge you to spend the extra five minutes you have, here and there throughout the day, reading the Bible and praying.

DO NOT STRESS OUT

People who are constantly on the go trying to "do this" and "be that" experience considerable stress. Some people do not realize it, but it can be stressful trying to be someone else. Imagine if an apple tree tried to produce grapes. It would still produce apples, but try to make them look like and smell like grapes. People do likewise with their lives. They try to fit in here and be accepted there, hoping it will gain them some benefit or advantage. This produces stress because you have to try to be someone else. In order to be yourself, you should not have to rehearse it. It should come naturally.

It is natural for a ball to roll down hill. If you want it to go in a direction other than down hill, you must exert some pressure upon it. When we try to be someone other than who God created us to be, we are exerting pressure. Pressure causes stress on the object being pressured and upon the one exerting the pressure upon it.

Stress is also caused by trying to go at a faster pace than designed. If we try to reach destinations in our lives ahead of season, there will be pressure involved. If we achieve it, we will not be ready to handle it, thereby exerting more pressure (stress) trying to maintain it. Society is in a race to achieve, discover, and arrive ahead of schedule. Someone may ask why walk when you can run? Another's response may be, why run if you are designed to walk?

BUSINESS WISDOM

The kingdom of heaven is like unto treasure hid in a field; that which when a man had found, he hideth, and for joy thereof goeth and selleth all that he hath, and buyeth that field. (Matthew 13:44 KJV)

Do not be overly anxious to run and tell everyone about your discovered treasure (favor, increase, riches, or prosperity). Sow (plant/hide) your treasure into the field (ground) that is producing for you. God uses what you have. In the scripture above, the man did not go sell the treasure to get money.

Once you start receiving increase, go after what is producing for you, not just the treasure itself. The scripture says that the man uses the treasure he has in order to obtain the field that was producing for him. Go after the field (the area, the ministry, or the environment) that is producing for you and in keeping with your personal destiny. The treasure is hid for you, not from you. Therefore, everyone else may not be experiencing the increase like you are.

Then Isaac sowed in that land, and received in the same year an hundredfold: and the Lord blessed him. (Genesis 26:12 KJV)

The Lord shall make thee plenteous in goods, in the fruit of thy body, and in the fruit of thy cattle, and in the fruit of thy ground, in the land which the Lord sware unto thy fathers to give thee. (Deuteronomy 28:11 KJV)

CHAPTER 6

THE MOMENTUM OF BEING DESTINY-MINDED

Your destiny should influence your choice of affiliations and associates. Almost every week or month someone asks, "What are you up to? What is going on?" People begin to relate to you or know you by what are doing or pursuing in life. Your destiny gives you zeal and purpose. It also helps defines the resources you need in life. God is obligated to supply your needs as you pursue your God-given purpose.

You should make it a priority to work towards your destiny on a regular basis. You should pray frequently about your destiny and apply personal commitment to see it through. Your destiny is yours. It is yours to nurture as well as defend. Life itself and people in life will challenge you concerning your destiny. Always be ready to give an answer for the hope that is within you.[80] During your private time, meditate upon your destiny and visualize yourself fulfilling it. Locate someone whom God is leading to fulfill a destiny similar to yours and learn from them. Establish yearly goals towards your destiny and hold yourself accountable. Tell others about your goals because their expectations will give you a sense of obligation to keep your word.

Establish your mind towards your destiny and value those whom God has placed in your life to counsel, help, and assist you. Focus on your God-given destiny and pursue it.

Halfway between here and there

Halfway between here and there is where many people stop, settle, or turn back. At halfway you no longer can embrace where you left, and you are yet to see your destination. Halfway is the point where the distance traveled equals the distance to go. However, one-step beyond halfway makes the remaining journey shorter than you have traveled. I wonder how many people reading this are halfway.

You may be weary because the journey has not revealed the fruit you envisioned. Perhaps your journey has been an uphill battle so far, and it seems (only seems) that if you turn around and go back at least it will be downhill. Do not go back! If your journey has been uphill, it means that you have developed the endurance for the remainder of the journey. It may seem as if you are in the middle of nowhere. You may simply be halfway.

Some people settle at halfway because it appears to be calm compared to what they have been through. If you have paused at halfway, do not settle there. Many people celebrate their accomplishments or achievements and set up camp based on what they have done, not realizing that they are only halfway. Even if you are ahead of the pack, do not assume you have won.

Our God-assigned tasks in life are based upon His intentions for us individually. Some of you may have begun to coast, thinking that you are near the end. You may be only halfway. Keep moving. A lukewarm Christian is a halfway Christian. They are halfway with their commitment to God. God says that He wishes that they were hot or cold.[81]

If you are halfway, it means that you are no longer visible from the starting point. Some of you may think that you are starting over after all these years. You are not starting over. You are starting from where you stopped. I believe you will experience a greater degree of God's anointing because you are not settling for halfway.

HE HAS ANOINTED YOU

The Spirit of the Lord is upon me, because He
has anointed me to…. (Luke 4:18 KJV)

Jesus was anointed to do the things mentioned in Luke 4:18-19. What has God anointed you to do? If you are not anointed to preach, it does not mean that you are not anointed. You are anointed to do something for God. The Spirit of the Lord is upon you because He has anointed you to fulfill your destiny. You need to live in constant awareness that the Spirit of the Lord is upon you, and He has anointed you.

You may be anointed to sing, organize, cook, sew, lead, run, serve, etc. Thank God that you are anointed. Now, use the anointing (the ability) He has given you (blessed you with). Spend time with God in order to discover what He has anointed you to do. If you try something and discover that you are not anointed to do it, do not let it end there. Remain in pursuit of your anointing.

One of the reasons why we experience poor service from others may be because they are not anointed to do it. If you are anointed to do something, you will have love and passion about doing it. You take it seriously, and you will do a good job. The result is that others will be blessed by your service because it is God working in you, helping you do it.

Every believer should say, "God has anointed me to …." We should discover and pursue what God has equipped us to do. You will not start as an expert, nor will you end being an expert. However, you will become progressively better. Why? Because you are anointed.

PEOPLE WHO EMPOWER YOU

There are people in the world and in your path whom God has empowered to empower you. I am not referring to them doing you a favor or promoting you, although it may result in such.

These people lighten up dark times in your life. Only five minutes with these people or with this person can do more for you than a year in the face of others. You should know who such a person is for your life.

You may see them occasionally. However, the occasion is very special. You love them with the love of God because you feel the love of God flowing through them into your life. It is worth your while to schedule time to call them or visit them. Because they refresh you, I believe that likewise you refresh them. This person may be younger than you, less educated than you or less fortunate than you, yet God uses them to build you. You need to accept whom God has appointed to help you.

If this relationship is of God, it cannot be over thrown.[82] They are not taking God's place in your life. They are assigned by God in your life to help you. They may not know their significance. The more you draw from them, the more apparent it will become to both of you. Such a person is designed by God. Therefore, they will not jeopardize your relationships with your spouse, children, and friends. God does everything decently and in order.[83] If you know whom God has equipped to empower you, call them or spend five minutes talking to them. Prove it for yourself.[84] Thank God for these people.

YOUR DESTINY AND ROYAL HERITAGE

But you are a chosen generation, a royal priesthood, a holy nation, a peculiar people. (1 Peter 2:9 KJV)

The decisions you make should be consistent with your destiny and your royal heritage. The major purchases you make should be consistent with your destiny and your royal heritage. The prayers you pray should be consistent with your destiny and your royal heritage. The battles you engage in should be consistent with your destiny and your royal heritage. Your attire should be consistent with your destiny and your royal heritage. The covenants and relationships you establish should be consistent with your destiny and your royal heritage. The words you speak and your confessions should be consistent with your destiny and your royal heritage.

Ensure your pursuits are consistent with your destiny and your royal heritage. Where you apply your energy and time should be consistent with your destiny and your royal heritage. Preserve your destiny and your royal heritage.

YOU ARE CLOSER NOW THAN YOU HAVE EVER BEEN

You are closer now to your destiny than you have ever been, although at times it looks like you are the farthest away from it and the least capable of reaching it. You are closer now than you were five years ago, one year ago, or last month. You have been pursuing for years, months, and weeks. You are so close to it that you can hear it and taste it. Previously it was not within view, but now it is not only within your view, it is within your reach. You can attain it, and you will attain it. You must maintain contact with it through your faith, confession, and perseverance. You must keep it in your view. The things you once hoped for are now within your grasp because you are closer now than you have ever been. The things which were far away are over the horizon.

You must prepare yourself for attainment. Make ready for attainment. Make ready to attain your goal. Get ready to possess your vision. When you are traveling on a journey in a car, as you approach your destination you prepare for arrival. You signal to others that you are exiting here in route to your destiny. At the end of your exit ramp, the traffic may become heavy. You slow down because now that you are closer to your destiny, there are turns you do not want to miss. At this point it is important to be in the proper lane. The direction sign may be smaller and in some instances, there are no signs and you must know (sense) where to turn.

As you approach the final turns, there are fewer people going your way. It may seem as if you are the only one traveling that direction. Even though you may love the journey, you must desire the destination more than the journey. Otherwise, you may keep traveling just to be traveling. Your destiny is a turn away, just around the corner, or one faith-fight away. You are closer now than you have ever been.

A FAITH-FIGHT AWAY

What if you knew that you were only one faith-fight away from your goal or objective? In the game of football, one first down can change the outcome of an entire game. I believe that every time we endure a faith-fight, God signals first down. The problem is that too often we punt on fourth or even third down because it seems as if we are not going to make it. We give up or give things over. I believe you are only a faith-fight away. The way to get a new set of downs is to use and apply the word of God to the situation.

Opposition may present a strong defense against you. Be persistent in the word of God, which you have practiced before the faith-fight. You are a faith-fight away from turning your entire season around for the good. Instead of being despondent about life in general, focus on and win every faith-fight you experience. Persevere and do not give up. The fight you are in is key and strategic for your victory in life. Keep fighting the good fight of faith, using the word of God.[85]

GOD ALWAYS WANTS YOU TO WIN

God always wants you to win. He did not create you for defeat. He created you to win. He is continually preparing you to win. Losing is not in God's nature. Therefore, He did not put defeat in you. There are times when you do not sense victory, and defeat seems unavoidable. Even then, and especially then, God wants you to win.

God made you a warrior and a fighter, one who does not surrender during the battle. Find a way to win in God. Be persistent in finding a way to win. Look for a way out of your circumstance. Look for a way to overcome what seems to be overcoming you. Find a way to make your marriage work. Find a way to forgive others. Find a way to get a job or get promoted. There is always a way. Those who persist will find it. They believe and plan like there is a possibility.

Avoid the "if this does not work out, I am quitting" syndrome. Give it all you have with what you have. If that does not work, try to try again. Sure, this has not worked and that did not work, but there is something that will work for you.

Find what gives you enthusiasm and stay with it. Some things give you momentary excitement. You want to pursue what gives you enthusiasm even during adversity, when others want to quit; you will endure any storm in order to maintain or attain. There is endurance and perseverance in you, but you have to find your niche which will pull those qualities to the surface.

You have what it takes to win, not at any and everything, but at what God destined for you. He put it in you to win. Your momentary setbacks are just as important as your victories. Your challenges are a necessary part of your life. Although they are unsightly, they are important. They shape, train, and point you in the right direction. Even when you have made the wrong choices, God will work with you to get you back on track. Remember that God always wants you to win, and He is working things for your good. Therefore, it is vital that you maintain your momentum.

ENDNOTES

[1] John 8:58

[2] Exodus 3:14

[3] Genesis 1:26

[4] 2 Corinthians 12:9

[5] 2 Corinthians 12:9

[6] Philippians 4:19

[7] John 3:16

[8] Romans 10:13

[9] 2 Peter 3:9

[10] John 1:46

[11] 2 Peter 3:9

[12] Colossians 4:17

[13] Exodus 4:10-17

[14] Psalm 121:2

[15] Hebrews 12:2

[16] Philippians 3:10

[17] Proverbs 26:22

[18] Psalm 23:5

[19] John 3:16, Romans 10:9

[20] John 1:1-12

[21] Exodus 3:12, Judges 6:12

[22] John 6:63

[23] Hebrews 4:12

[24] Psalm 119:130

[25] Joshua 1:8

[26] James 1:22

[27] Revelation 3:20

[28] Exodus 3:2-3

[29] Jonah 1:17

[30] Acts 9:3

[31] I Kings 19:12

[32] 1 John 5:14-15

[33] 1 Corinthians 14:4, Jude 20

[34] 1 Corinthians 2:11

[35] Luke 11:5-13, 18:1-5

[36] Luke 18:1

[37] 1 Thessalonians 5:17

[38] Psalm 63:1

[39] 1 John 1:9, Ephesians 4:32, Matthew 5:44

[40] Mark 12:30

[41] John 10:10, 3John 2

[42] John 3:16

[43] John 15:13

[44] Exodus 20:5

[45] 1 Corinthians 15:10

[46] 2 Corinthians 12:9

[47] 2 Corinthians 12:9

[48] 1 Corinthians 15:10

[49] Luke 12:48

[50] Galatians 2:21

[51] James 4:6

[52] Mark 4:35-41

[53] Mark 4:38

[54] Colossians 3:15

[55] Galatians 5:7

[56] 1 Corinthians 1:25

[57] Hebrews 12:2-3

[58] Galatians 6:9

[59] John 11:25

[60] John 14:17

[61] John 14:16

[62] Job 33:4

[63] John 16:13

[64] Ephesians 6:10

[65] 2 Corinthians 4:16

[66] Hebrews 13:8

[67] Romans 5:17

[68] John 10:10

[69] 2 Corinthians 2:14

[70] 1 Corinthians 15:57

[71] 1 Corinthians 15:58

[72] Psalm 103:20

[73] James 2:20

[74] Ephesians 5:25

[75] Matthew 19:5

[76] 1 John 5:14-15

[77] 1 Peter 1:15

[78] 2 Corinthians 4:7

[79] Haggai 1:5-7

[80] 1 Peter 3:15

[81] Revelation 3:15-16

[82] Acts 5:39

[83] 1 Corinthians 14:40

[84] 1 Thessalonians 5:21

[85] 1 Timothy 6:12

Author Contact Information

Robert L. Smith
P.O. Box 31603
Alexandria, VA 22310
Email: SROBERTL@VERIZON.NET

Author Product Information

Book: *You Are in Great Demand*, Insight Publishing Group, 2005